Nature's Footprints

IN THE
DESERT

By Q. L. Pearce and W. J. Pearce

Illustrated by Delana Bettoli

Silver Press

For my husband
Ralph Coyote
—D.B.

10   9   8   7   6   5   4   3   2   1

Library of Congress Cataloging-in-Publication Data

Pearce, Q. L. (Querida Lee) Nature's footprints in the desert / by Q. L. Pearce and W. J. Pearce; pictures by Delana Betolli. p.   cm. Summary: Briefly describes the behavior of such desert animals as the tortoise, prairie dog, gila monster, and coyote.   1. Desert fauna—Juvenile literature.   2 Desert fauna—North America—Juvenile literature.   [1. Desert animals.]   I. Pearce, W. J. (William Julian), 1952-   II. Bettoli, Delana, ill.   III. Title.
QL116.P43   1990
591.909′54—dc20
89-39507
CIP
AC
ISBN 0-671-68829-4   ISBN 0-671-68825-1 (lib. bgd.)

A Note to Parents

NATURE'S FOOTPRINTS is a read-aloud picture book series that introduces children to a wide variety of animals in a unique, interactive way.

Ten animals are presented in pairs, along with a sample of each animal's footprints. In the scene that follows, the animals can be found by tracking the paths of their footprints, thereby building your child's observational skill in a lively, fun format.

Detailed illustrations and text provide more information about the animals. Encourage your child to point out details about the animals and their environment.

Accompanying the NATURE'S FOOTPRINTS series is the NATURE'S FOOTPRINTS FIELD GUIDE—a handy, colorful reference guide that teaches children even more about the animals in this series.

THE TORTOISE

The desert tortoise moves slowly.

It carries its heavy shell on its back.

This tortoise eats dry desert grass and plants.

THE VULTURE

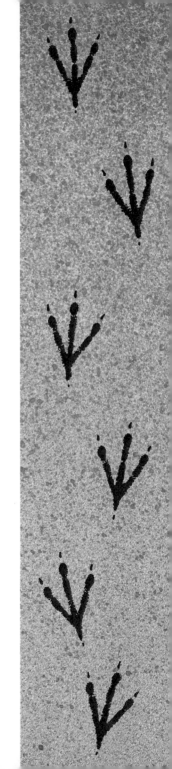

The vulture flies high in the sky.

This big bird watches the ground for a meal.

It eats meat left behind by other animals.

The tortoise lives in a shady burrow.

Follow nature's footprints.

They will lead you to the half-hidden tortoise.

The vulture must share its meal with others.
Follow nature's footprints.
They will lead you to the hungriest vulture.

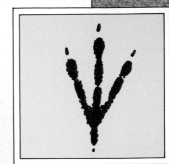

THE ROADRUNNER

The roadrunner would rather run than fly.

It can run faster than a human.

This speedy bird eats insects and tiny lizards.

THE PRAIRIE DOG

The prairie dog never strays far from its burrow.

It scampers out to nibble grass and weeds.

At the first sign of danger, it dashes back to safety.

The roadrunner builds its nest near the ground.

Follow nature's footprints.

They will lead you to the skillful roadrunner.

Prairie dogs bark a warning when danger is near.
Follow nature's footprints.
They will lead you to the noisy prairie dog.

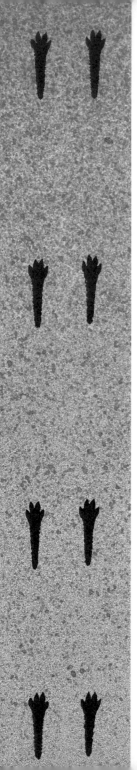

THE KANGAROO RAT

The kangaroo rat hops from place to place.

It does not need to drink water.

It gets water from the seeds it eats.

THE HARE

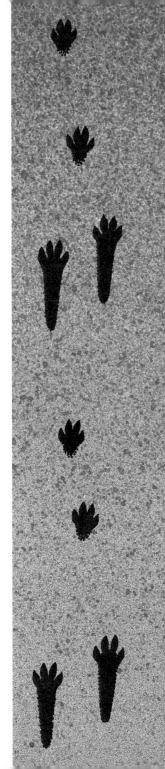

The jackrabbit is a speedy desert hare.

It has many enemies, including the coyote and the hawk.

The jackrabbit escapes its enemies by leaping away.

The kangaroo rat often stores its seeds.
Follow nature's footprints.
They will lead you to the busy kangaroo rat.

Leaves and grass are the jackrabbit's favorite food.
Follow nature's footprints.
They will lead you to the hungry jackrabbit.

THE GILA MONSTER

The slow-moving Gila (HEE-luh) monster is a lizard.

It hides in its burrow from the hot sun.

At night, this lizard searches for eggs and insects to eat.

THE RATTLESNAKE

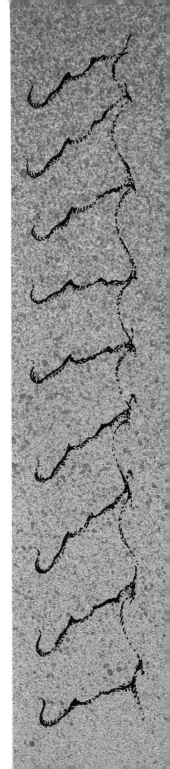

The rattlesnake slithers across the ground on its belly.

This scaly reptile eats lizards and mice.

It swallows its meal in one bite.

The Gila monster has a poisonous bite.
Follow nature's footprints.
They will lead you to the colorful Gila monster.

The rattlesnake often hunts at night.

Follow nature's footprints.

They will lead you to the searching rattlesnake.

THE BOBCAT

The bobcat is very sure-footed.

It prowls at night in its rocky desert home.

The bobcat hunts for rabbits, mice, and birds.

THE COYOTE

The clever coyote hunts at night.

Rabbits, lizards, and mice are its favorite food.

The coyote may travel many miles to find a meal!

The bobcat depends on surprise to capture its meal.
Follow nature's footprints.
They will lead you to the sneaky bobcat.

The lone coyote cries, "*Ahooooooo!*"
Follow nature's footprints.
They will lead you to the howling coyote.